I0137516

Tasty Treats by Tea Time

A Collection of Recipes by
Dena Macklin & Chris Jennings

Published by:
ATR Publishing

Cover Photo by:
Macklin Photography
http://www.flickr.com/photos/robmacklin/

Back Cover Photo by:
Macklin Photography
http://www.flickr.com/photos/robmacklin/

About Us

We are Dena Macklin and Chris Jennings. We never dreamed we would open and own our own tearoom. We look back at the series of events that lead us to this opportunity. It has been a wonderful journey for both of us. We are so thankful to Amy Lawrence of An Afternoon to Remember. She hired two stay at home moms to help run her kitchen at An Afternoon to Remember Fine Tea and Gifts in Newcastle, CA. She took a big chance on us! She gave us the tools we needed to open our own tearoom, teaching us by her example. We thank her for all she has done for us over the years! Her wonderful scone recipe is the base to all of our scone recipes now! It has become a treasured recipe by all who loved her tearoom and now those who visit ours.

It is hard to believe it has been two years since we opened the doors here at Tea Time on October 22, 2010! In many ways it feels like time has flown by so quickly. Yet we have savored each day and every special moment with our dear customers! Thank you to all of our customers for supporting us and helping make Tea Time a successful business. It is your faithful business that keeps us open and encourages us daily! We see the smiles and hear the laughter in our tearoom and it gives us great joy! It has always been our desire to provide a place of respite and refreshing. We hope when you enter the doors you feel comforted by the charm of the Old Victorian and the smells of the freshly baked treats. We have compiled some of our most requested recipes and we hope it will be something you enjoy over the years. Remember to take

About Us Continued

moments in your everyday life to fill a teapot, bake some hot scones, and just sit and relax with someone you love in the comfort of your own home. It's these simple gestures in life that can bring so much joy to the ones you love.

Again, our greatest thanks and appreciation to each of you.

Dena and Chris

Table of Contents

Table of Contents Continued

Soups, Salads, Quiche
Brunch

Tuscan Tomato Soup

- 3 Tbsp olive oil
- 1 yellow onion chopped
- 1 clove of garlic minced or you can cheat and use ½ tsp of chopped garlic from a jar
- 1 can whole quality plum tomatoes (28 ounces)
- 1½ Tbsp paprika or cumin
- 2¾ cups vegetable or chicken broth
- ½ cup white wine (we use a sweet white wine such as Moscato in our soup)
- 2 tsp lemon juice
- 1 tsp pepper (or to your taste)
- ½ tsp salt (or to your taste)
- 2 tsp fresh chopped basil
- 1 tsp fresh chopped thyme
- 1 tsp fresh chopped rosemary

If you are low on time you can substitute the fresh herbs with 1 Tbsp dry Italian Seasoning

- 1 jar of roasted red pepper
- 1 can of northern white beans (it depends on how many you like in your soup but if you want more add an additional can of beans)
- 1 can of sweet corn (freshly cooked or frozen corn can be used as well)
- ½ bag of potatoes (frozen work well in this soup)

Notes

Tuscan Tomato Soup Continued

If you prefer freshly cooked potatoes you can boil any variety of potato and cube into small size pieces and add to the soup at the end after they have cooled. In a heavy 3 quart pan over medium heat, add olive oil and onion and stir till soft (approximately 4 minutes). Add garlic and stir for an additional minute. Add the roasted red peppers and plum tomatoes along with the juice of the tomatoes. Add the spice, herbs, salt, and pepper to the mixture and let simmer on low heat for about 4 minutes. In a blender or food processor purée the soup in small batches until smooth and creamy in texture. Return the purée to the cooking pan and add the broth, lemon juice, and the sweet white wine. Add the can of beans and corn to the mixture. Stir over the medium heat until hot. Pour into small cups and garnish with a dollop of sour cream or crème fraiche. Garnish with a sprig of parsley. We hope you enjoy!

Makes approximately 35 (½ cup serving portions) of soup

Notes

Roasted Vegetable Soup

- 1 large sweet yellow onion
- 1 cup potatoes peeled and cubed (frozen pre-cubed potatoes are a good substitute for quicker preparation if you have limited time to prepare your meal.)
- 1 cup yams peeled and cubed (frozen pre-cubed yams work just fine – let them thaw for 20 minutes before adding them to the baking dish).
- 4 ribs of celery
- ½ cup cauliflower cut into bits
- 3 Tbsp olive oil
- ½ tsp of salt
- ½ tsp pepper
- 2 tsp Italian seasoning
- 6 cups vegetable broth or chicken broth

Preheat your oven to 400°. Place vegetables on the prepared baking sheet (jelly roll or 9 x 13 baking dish) lined with foil. Toss all of the vegetables with olive oil until well coated. Sprinkle on the salt, pepper, and Italian seasoning mixture. Mix again with your hands until all the veggies are well coated. Don't be afraid to get a little messy! Place the vegetable in the oven and roast them for 30 – 40 minutes (ovens vary on temperature and times). Pull them from oven and scoop them into a large stock pot that has the vegetable or chicken broth already in it. Bring mixture to a boil and then reduce the heat to a simmer (low heat). Cover the pot and let

Notes

Roasted Vegetable Soup Continued

it cook for 30 minutes. Transfer to a blender or food processor (or use an immersion blender). Blend until very smooth. Pour into small bowls and garnish with a dollop of sour cream or plain yogurt. Top with a sprig of parsley or basil! Enjoy!

Makes approximately 40 (½ cup serving portions)

Try this with "Dena's Homemade Cornbread" (page 33) for a delicious combination!

Notes

Fresh Strawberry Spiced Soup

- 64 ounce container of strawberry yogurt (any brand works just fine)
- ¾ cup of apple cider
- 2 tsp of cinnamon
- ¼ cup pure honey (we love to use orange blossom honey)
- ¾ cup fresh strawberries

Chop strawberries into small chunks. Place the fresh strawberries into the food processor with the apple juice and pulse for 3 minutes. Add the yogurt, cinnamon, and honey to the processor. Run on high speed for 5 minutes until smooth and creamy in texture. Pour into small cups or bowls. Garnish with a freshly sliced strawberry. Drizzle honey over the strawberry in a zigzag pattern. Enjoy!

Makes 20 (½ cup serving size) portions of cold soup

Notes

Sweet Potato Pumpkin Soup

- 5 cups boiling water
- 2 Knorr® chicken or vegetable bouillon cubes (you can substitute 5 cups can or boxed chicken or vegetable broth)
- 1 cup white wine (Chardonnay is recommended but in a pinch you can use other white wines)
- ½ cup honey
- 1 can yams (40 ounces)
- 1 can solid pack pumpkin purée (no spices, small can)
- 2 Tbsp Italian seasoning
- 2 tsp pepper
- ½ tsp salt (or to your own taste)
- 2 tsp cinnamon

Combine the 5 cups boiling water with the 2 cubes of bouillon...whisk to combine.

Place yams (with their juice from can) into a blender (or use an emulsion blender in a large bowl). Add 3 cups of the broth, italian seasoning, pepper, salt, and cinnamon to the blender. Puree the ingredients together for 2 minutes until smooth and creamy. Add pumpkin purée, the rest of the broth, wine, and honey to a stock pot or crock pot. Cook on low simmer in the stock pot. High setting in crock pot for 1 hour...then reduce to low for 2 more hours. If cooking on the stove top stir with a whisk off and on to keep it from scorching. Cook for 25-30 minutes low-medium heat on stove top.

Notes

Sweet Potato Pumpkin Soup Continued

Pour into mini cups or bowls and garnish with a dollop of sour cream and chopped chives.

Perfect with "Roasted Red Pepper and Artichoke Quiche" (page 25)

Makes 20 mini cups of soup

Notes

Simple Marinated Green Bean Salad

- 1 cup blanched green beans (or as a quick substitute you can use frozen green beans – 16 oz. bag)
- 4 Tbsp olive oil
- 2½ Tbsp white balsamic vinegar
- ½ tsp Dijon mustard
- ½ tsp sugar
- ½ tsp Italian seasoning
- ½ tsp pepper
- ½ tsp salt (or salt alternative)
- 1 lime
- ½ cup toasted chopped pecans (or walnuts)

Place fresh green beans in salted boiling water for 15 minutes. Drain and let rest.

Place all the ingredients except for the nuts in a gallon sized plastic bag. Seal and turn the bag several times to mix the ingredients. Refrigerate for several hours to marinate the beans. Drain the marinade and place green beans in a bowl and squeeze one lime over the beans then sprinkle with the toasted nuts.

Toasted Nuts:

Chop the nuts and place them on a parchment lined baking sheet in a 350 degree oven for 10-15 minutes. Watch closely for light browning. Pull from oven and let rest for 20 minutes and then top your salad! Enjoy!

Makes approximately 12 (½ cup serving portions)

Notes

Roasted Red Pepper and Artichoke Quiche

- 2 cans of quartered (non-marinated) Artichoke hearts
- 1 jar of Roasted Red Peppers
- 2 large bags of shredded three cheese blend (approximately 2 cups each pie)
- I container or dried onions (1 ½ tsp each of dried onion per pie)

"Dena's "Don't Be Intimidated" Pie Crust" (page 95) is a perfect crust for this quiche or you can purchase a pre made pie crust (either frozen or rolled dough from refrigerator section). Allow frozen crusts to thaw overnight in the refrigerator. Bake the crusts for 12-15 minutes (par – bake them until light brown)

Pull from the oven and let rest for 15 minutes. Prepare your "Quiche Batter" (page 29).

Filling:

Drain and chop the artichokes and red peppers into small pieces

Put a thin layer of the three cheese blend on the bottom of the pie crust. Sprinkle the dried onion over the cheese layer (approximately 1½ tsp of the dried onion). Add in your artichokes and roasted red peppers. Layer the shredded cheese blend on top of the artichokes and red peppers (approximately ¾ cup). Fill the cheese to just below the pie crust edge. Pour the well whisked batter into the filled pie crusts until just to the crust edge. Pour a little and then let it settle.

Notes

Roasted Red Pepper and Artichoke Quiche
Continued

Keep pouring until it's full and settled completely. Line the edge of the crust with foil strips or pie crust covers. We discovered this wonderful invention at a kitchen supply store! It's simple and easy to use. It's a solid ring that covers the whole circumference of the pie. Place the quiche in a pre heated 350 degree oven and bake for 1 hour 10 minutes. Check it as you bake it. You may need to add an additional 15-20 minutes. You will know it's done if it's lightly browned on top and firm when you jiggle it lightly. Pull from the oven and let them rest on a cutting board or cooling rack. Serve warm and/or freeze the remaining quiche. Wrap thoroughly in foil and place in a freezer safe storage bag.

Makes 4 quiche

Notes

Quiche Batter

This recipe makes enough batter to make 4 quiche. You can make the quiche and let them cool completely. Enjoy one and wrap the remaining three quiche in foil and place them in the freezer for later use. They will hold in the freezer for up to 6 months. It's preferable to use them within 3 months.

- 9 eggs
- 1¼ cup whole vitamin D milk (preferred but even low fat milk can be substituted if you are cutting back)
- 1¼ cup whole whipping cream
- ¼ cup self-rising flour (If you don't have this on hand you can substitute all-purpose flour with ¼ tsp baking powder, ⅛ tsp baking soda, and ⅛ tsp salt with the ¼ cup flour)
- 1 tsp Italian Seasoning

We have found a trick to making our quiche light and fluffy. Place the whipping cream, milk, Italian seasoning, and flour into a food processor or blender. Blend on high speed for 2-4 minutes. Watch it closely as you do not want to turn your liquid whipping cream into firm whip cream. If you turn it into whip cream do not panic. We have made this error and you can safely use it by adding it to the egg mixture and letting it settle for 20 minutes. It's best to try and catch it before this occurs. In the stand mixer add all of your eggs and using the whisk attachment...whisk until thoroughly smooth and creamy. Pour the milk/cream mixture into the egg batter. Whisk for 3-5 minutes until thoroughly combined and very smooth in texture. We like to use plastic pitchers with

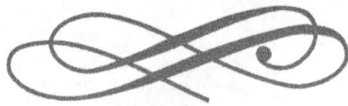

Notes

Quiche Batter Continued

a spout for pouring the batter into our prepared pie crusts/-filling. The spout on the plastic pitcher makes for easy pouring of the liquid batter. See the "Roasted Red Pepper and Artichoke Quiche Recipe" for the full recipe.

If you ever have extra batter left over you can safely freeze the remainder in a plastic freezer safe bag or a plastic tupperware container for later use. Just thaw overnight and whisk either in a mixer or by hand.

Makes 4 quiche

Notes

Dena's Homemade Cornbread

- 1½ cups all-purpose flour
- ½ cup corn meal
- 1 cup sugar
- 1¼ Tbsp baking powder
- ½ tsp salt
- 1¼ cups milk
- 2 large eggs (lightly beaten)
- ⅓ cup vegetable or canola oil
- 3 Tbsp melted butter (unsalted)
- ⅔ cup frozen corn or canned corn
- For a savory option add 2 tsp of dried Italian seasoning to the batter.

Preheat your oven to 350°. Spray your baking pan with non-stick flour spray. Pam makes a great one. You can also use muffin tins with cupcake liners for muffins.

Combine the dry ingredients in a bowl. Add milk, lightly beaten eggs, oil, and butter to the dry ingredients and whisk by hand (do not use an electic mixer when making this batter). Fold the corn and savory seasoning into the batter. Pour the batter into prepared baking pan. You can use a square 9 x 9 glass pan, or a deep dish pie plate, or muffin cups. Bake approximately 18 minutes for muffins. An additional 5-8 minutes for the baking pans. Keep an eye on it and check with a knife inserted in the center of the pan or muffins. Serve warm! Delicious with honey butter or even maple syrup!

Makes 8 generous slices

Notes

Dena's Gluten-Free Cornbread

Dena's son was recently put on a gluten-free diet due to food allergies. It has greatly improved his health but he has had to let go of some of his favorite treats because of it. It's now her mission as his mom to take some of his old favorite treats and transform them into a gluten-free variety. His favorite one so far is Dena's Gluten-Free Cornbread derived from the recipe "Dena's Homemade Cornbread" (page 33). If you or someone you love is gluten-free now, I hope these recipes will satisfy their craving for an old style treat without cheating on their gluten-free diet.

- 1 cup Gluten-Free All Purpose Baking Mix (I discovered this wonderful item at Sprouts Market)
- ¾ cup corn meal (my son is able to tolerate Quaker® brand corn meal but others with celiac may prefer Bob's Red Mill® – found at Whole Foods®, Trader Joe's®, Sprouts®, and many health food stores).
- 1 cup sugar
- 1 Tbsp baking powder (if needed there is gluten-free baking powder available at the above stores)
- ½ tsp salt
- 1 cup milk
- 2 large eggs (slightly beaten
- ⅓ cup vegetable oil (or canola)
- 3 Tbsp melted butter (unsalted)
- ½ cup frozen or canned corn

Notes

Dena's Gluten-Free Cornbread Continued

Tips:

- If you cannot locate the gluten-free baking mix you can make your own using ¼ cup rice flour, 1 cup whole grain sorghum flour, and ¼ cup tapioca starch flour (combine all three flours).

Preheat oven to 350°. Spray your baking pan (9x9 square or deep dish pie plate) with non stick canola spray (no flour).

Combine the dry ingredients. Whisk well. Add the milk, eggs, oil, and butter. Mix by hand (do not use an electric mixer for this recipe). Fold in the corn as your last step. The mixture will be slightly thick. Do not let it sit for long as the rice flour in the baking mix will absorb the liquid and turn very thick. Pour batter into the pan as soon as you can and sprinkle the top lightly with regular sugar. This makes a sweet crunch on top of your bread. Bake for 20-26 minutes (depends on your oven). The best thing is to watch it for browning on the top and check the center with a knife for doneness. Pull from oven when no batter is left on your knife when checking it. Serve warm with butter and honey! Yum! Even non-gluten-free eaters will love this one!

Makes 8 generous slices

Notes

Christmas Baked French Toast

This has become a Christmas tradition at Dena's house.

- 1 loaf of sweet French bread (I prefer the pre-sliced option)
- 8 large eggs
- 1 cup half and half
- 1 cup whole whipping cream
- 1 cup whole milk
- ½ cup sugar
- 1½ tsp pure vanilla extract
- ½ tsp cinnamon
- ½ tsp. nutmeg
- ¼ tsp salt

Prepare the batter first. Combine the eggs, half and half, cream, milk, sugar, vanilla, spices, and salt. You can use a hand held mixer or a stand mixer to combine your ingredients. Be careful not to overbeat as the whipping cream will become stiff and you don t want butter from it. Mix until combined. In a large baking pan (9 x 13) spray it well with a non stick flour spray. Pour a small amount of the batter in the baking pan. Spread it around with a spatula. Layer the sliced French bread over the batter. Cover the whole bottom of your pan with sliced bread. Pour another light amount of batter over the bread. Spread again with spatula. Add another layer of the sliced bread on top of the first layer. Pour the remainder of the batter over the bread. Make sure with this last layer of batter that it thoroughly covers the

Notes

Christmas Baked French Toast Continued

bread. Cover the pan with foil and refrigerate it overnight. The next day you will need to preheat your oven to 350°.

Bake at 350° for 40 minutes. During the last 10 minutes of baking time sprinkle ¾ cup brown sugar over the top of the French toast. Serve with "Orange White Chocolate Sauce" (page 43).

Makes approximately 8 large portions

Notes

Orange White Chocolate Sauce

- ⅔ cup heavy whipping cream
- ¾ cup butter
- 3 Tbsp sugar
- 6 ounces white chocolate chips (use a good quality chip like Ghiradelli® or Nestle®)
- Finely grate the rind of one large orange
- 3 Tbsp orange liquor

Heat the cream and butter in a microwave safe bowl for 2-3 minutes. Stirring after each minute with a fork or whisk.

Add the sugar and white chips and whisk. Heat an additional 1-2 minutes. Whisk after each minute.

After whisking the sugar and white chips...add the orange zest and the orange liquor. In a pinch you can substitute orange juice for the liquor. Whisk the final ingredients well.

If the mixture firms up after cooling down you can microwave it an additional 30-60 seconds to make it smooth and pourable.

Pour over your favorite cobbler, pie, ice cream, and French toast! Enjoy!

TIP:

Large microwave ovens are typically hotter than on the counter versions. Turn your power setting down to 50% on large microwaves.

Notes

Tea Sandwich Spreads

Spinach Artichoke Spread

- 1 pkg frozen chopped spinach thawed and drained
- 1 can artichoke hearts drained and chopped
- 2 8 ounce packages of cream cheese
- ½ cup parmesan cheese
- 1 or 2 cloves of freshly pressed garlic (for a quick alternative you can use 1 or 2 tsp of minced garlic in a jar)
- Dash of salt and pepper (to your taste preference)

Mix cream cheese and sour cream together in food processor. Add the remaining ingredients. Pulse to combine. Spread on your favorite choice of bread. Example: dark rye, sourdough, buttermilk bread, dill rye, honey wheat. Cut into the shape you desire. Garnish with shredded parmesan cheese and a fresh spinach leaf or use a fresh slice of cucumber or tomato. Be creative!

Makes approximately 60 tea sandwiches (small fingers)

Notes

Roasted Pecan Pimento Pepper Spread

- 1 8 ounce package cream cheese (softened)
- ¾ cup roasted pecans (you can roast your own pecans in a 350 degree oven for 15-18 minutes – pre chop your nuts and place them on a parchment lined cookie sheet. Watch them as you roast them. Let them cool for 15 minutes before using in the spread).
- ¼ cup green pepper, chopped finely
- ¼ cup sweet onion, chopped finely
- 3 Tbsp chopped pimento
- 1 Tbsp catsup
- Pinch of salt and pepper (to your taste)

Pulse the cream cheese until smooth. Add the remaining ingredients to processor and pulse to combine well. Spread on your choice of bread and cut into fingers. Garnish with a roasted pecan or a slice of green pepper. Enjoy!

Makes approximately 32 tea sandwiches

Notes

Feta Cheese Spread

- 1 8 ounce package cream cheese (softened)
- ½ cup sour cream
- 1 4 ounce container of feta cheese crumble
- ¼ cup unsalted butter (softened)
- ¼ cup chopped ripe olives
- 2 Tbsp finely chopped green onions
- ¼ cup parsley finely chopped (in a pinch you can substitute dried parsley)

Place the cream cheese and butter into the food processor and run until creamy and smooth. Add the remaining ingredients and pulse until combined well. Spread the mixture on your favorite bread and cut into squares or fingers. Garnish with parsley or toasted, slivered almonds.

Makes approximately 32 tea sandwiches

Notes

Corn Fiesta Cups

- 2 cans Mexican corn (drained well)
- 1 small can chopped black olives
- 1 small can chopped green chillies
- 1 small bunch of green onions chopped
- 12 ounces of shredded cheddar cheese
- 12 ounces cream cheese (1½ packages)
- ½ cup sour cream
- 1 Tbsp garlic powder
- 1 Tbsp Accent
- 1 bag of Tostitos® Scoops Tortilla Chips

Mix cream cheese and sour cream together in food processor. Add all of the rest of the ingredients and pulse to combine or fold in with a large spoon. Scoop with a cookie scooper into individual Tostitos Scoops Tortilla Chips. Sprinkle the top of each cup with shredded cheddar cheese.

Makes 55 individual Corn Fiesta Cups

This makes a great appetizer too!

Notes

Desserts

Strawberry Cupcakes

- 1 box of strawberry cake mix (we usually use Betty Crocker® or Duncan Hines®)
- 1 lg package instant vanilla pudding
- 1 cup buttermilk
- 4 eggs
- ½ cup vegetable or canola oil
- ½ cup water
- ⅔ cup fresh strawberries puréed in a food processor or finely chopped

Preheat oven to 350°. Beat together the cake mix, pudding, buttermilk, eggs, oil, and water with an electric mixer at medium speed. Fold in the fresh strawberry purée. Line muffin pans with cupcake liners. Fill each cup about half full. You can also make a 10 inch Classic Crown Bundt pan style cake with this batter. Once it is baked, slice it and drizzle melted white chocolate over it for a decorative and yummy touch. Baking time for Bundt pan is approximately 25 minutes.

Bake the muffins for 9-12 minutes (depending on your oven). Keep an eye on them. Lightly touch the center of one cupcake to see if it's firm to the touch but not overly cooked. You want them moist, not over-done. I watch mine like a mother hawk! Pull them from oven when done and set out to rest for 10 minutes then flip onto a tray or cutting board. Let them cool thoroughly before piping them with "Dena's Butter Cream Frosting" (page 101)! Once they are cooled and frosted top them with a fresh slice of strawberry for garnish. Enjoy!

Makes 45 cupcakes

Notes

Caramel Apple Cupcakes

- 1 box yellow cake mix
- 3 eggs
- 1 can apple pie filling (seasonally you can find caramel apple pie filling too as great alternative)
- 3 Tbsp caramel sauce (if using regular apple pie filling)
- 3 Tbsp Best Foods Mayonaise
- 1 tsp. pumpkin pie alternative

In stand mixer combine the yellow cake mix with the 3 eggs, 3 Tbsp mayo,1 tsp pumpkin pie spice, 3 Tbsp caramel sauce, and the can of apple pie filling. Run on low speed for 2 minutes.

Scoop mixture with an ice cream scooper into cupcake lined pans. Bake at 350° for 12-15 minutes (depending on your oven temperatures). Test the center of one cupcake with a toothpick or thin knife. Frost with "Cream Cheese Frosting" (page 109) when completely cooled. Drizzle caramel sauce over the frosted cupcakes as a beautiful garnish!

Makes approximately 1 dozen cupcakes/2 dozen mini cupcakes

Notes

Chris' Peanut Butter Gluten-Free Cookies

- 1 16 ounce jar of chunky peanut butter (we love Skippy® Roasted Honey Nut Super Chunk)
- 2 eggs
- 2 cups sugar
- 1 tsp baking soda
- 1 tsp pure vanilla extract

Empty the jar of chunky peanut butter into your mixer. Add the eggs, sugar, soda, and vanilla. Mix until well combined.

Scoop using a cookie scoop onto a cutting board or plastic tray. Place in the freezer for 1 hour to firm the balls and move them to a zip lock freezer bag for future use.

To bake:

Pre heat your oven to 350°. Place 20 cookies on a parchment lined cookie sheet. Sprinkle each cookie ball with generous amount of sugar and press with a glass. Bake for 7-8 minutes. Be careful not to over bake these. They cook quickly. These taste just like your grandma's old fashioned peanut butter cookie! It's hard to believe they are gluten-free too!

Makes 2 dozen cookies.

Notes

Chocolate Peppermint Shortbread Tea Cookies

- 2 cups unsalted butter
- 1 cup sugar
- 2 tsp pure vanilla extract
- 4 cups flour
- 1½ cups milk chocolate chips
- ¾ cup chocolate peppermint black tea (pulse in a food processor until smaller in size)

Preheat oven to 350°. Beat butter, sugar, and vanilla in a mixing bowl. Add the flour mixture and mix on medium speed until all of the dough comes together. Add the 1½ cups milk chocolate and ¼ cup chocolate peppermint black tea until well combined. Beat on low to medium speed until it's evenly incorporated into the dough.

Scoop into balls with a cookie scoop onto a parchment lined baking sheet. Sprinkle with regular sugar and press with the bottom of a glass cup. Bake for 8-12 minutes until lightly browned. Keep an eye on them. It's best to not overcook these as you want them lightly brown and delicate in texture.

Let them cool.

If you want to garnish them, you can drizzle melted chocolate over the tops in a zig zag pattern or dip them in melted chocolate. You can also garnish them with half of an Andes Mint or sprig of fresh mint placed in the center of your cookie. Place them in the refrigerator to set the chocolate drizzle.

Makes approximately 80 cookies

Notes

Lemon or Strawberry Bars

- 1 lemon or strawberry cake mix (we prefer Duncan Hines®)
- 4 eggs
- 1 can of lemon or lime pie filling

Frosting:

- 8 ounces cream cheese (softened)
- 1 stick of unsalted butter (softened)
- 4 cups powdered sugar
- 1 tsp pure vanilla extract

Using a mixer combine the cake mix with the eggs. Fold in the pie filling with a large spatula. Thoroughly spray a jelly roll pan with non stick baking/flour spray. Using a spatula fold the mixture into the baking pan. Spread it out evenly. It takes a little work to smooth it out to the corners. Stick with it.

Place in a 350 degree preheated oven. Bake for 15 minutes (depending on your oven variation). Use a knife inserted in the center to check for doneness. Pull from oven and let rest in the fridge for 30 minutes.

Frosting:

Whip the cream cheese and butter using a mixer. Turn mixer down and add the powdered sugar and vanilla extract. Turn up to high speed once powdered sugar is combined. Whip until smooth and creamy. Spread on top of the cooled cake.

We like to place the cake in the freezer (covered with a

Notes

Lemon or Strawberry Bars Continued

second jelly roll pan and wrapped with saran wrap to secure it). Freeze over night and pull out to cut it into bars.

Makes approximately 24 pieces (depending on the size of the bar you would like)

Tips:

If you want to get fancy you can also garnish each bar with a sliver of lemon or a slice of strawberry.

Notes

Chris' Old Fashioned Chocolate Cake

- 2 sticks of unsalted butter
- 1 cup of water
- 2 eggs
- 4 Tbsp cocoa
- 1 tsp salt
- 1 tsp baking soda
- 2 cups sugar
- 2 cups flour
- ½ cup sour cream

Frosting:

- 1 stick of unsalted butter
- 4 rounded Tbsp of cocoa powder
- 1 8 ounce package softened cream cheese
- 1 lb powdered sugar
- 1 tsp pure vanilla extract

Place the butter, water, and cocoa in a saucepan and bring up to a boil. Stirring as you bring it to a boil. Remove from the stove once it reaches a boil. Add sugar, flour, baking soda, salt, and eggs. Stir ingredients by hand until well blended. Stir in the sour cream. Pour mixture into a 9 x 12 inch baking pan (spray pan with a non stick baking spray with flour) and bake at 350° for 20-25 minutes. Use a knife in the center to check for doneness. Cool and set aside while making frosting.

Frosting:

Notes

Chris' Old Fashioned Chocolate Cake
Continued

Place butter, cocoa powder and cream cheese into a saucepan and bring to a boil. Using a whisk stir as it heats to a boil. Once it reaches a boil remove from the heat and add 1 lb powdered sugar and 1 tsp pure vanilla extract. Spread the mixture over the cake while hot and sprinkle with your favorite nuts (pecans or walnuts).

Makes approximately 12 large pieces of cake and 24 small squares of cake.

Notes

Homemade Carrot Cake

- 5 eggs
- 1¾ cups sugar
- 2½ cups cake flour
- 3 tsp cinnamon
- 2 tsp baking soda
- 1 tsp salt
- 2½ cups grated carrots (you can cheat and purchase pre-grated carrots in a bag at the grocery store)
- 1¼ cups finely chopped fresh pineapple (or cheat and use a can of crushed pineapple)
- 1¼ cups currants or raisins
- ½ cup finely chopped pecans (or walnuts) – I like to finely chop mine in a food processor.

Mix together eggs and sugar on medium speed of stand mixer.

In a separate bowl prepare the dry ingredients and in another bowl combine the carrots, fruits and nuts (optional).

Add the dry ingredients to the eggs and sugar and combine using low speed on mixer. Then add in your carrots, pineapple, raisins, and pecans. Low speed until combined. As your final step slowly stream in 1¾ cups vegetable or canola oil.

Pour into prepared pans (spray well with non-stick baking spray) and bake at 350° for 45 minutes-1 hour. Check at 30 minutes as ovens vary on baking times. Use the knife test in center of cake to test for doneness. Remove and cool for

Notes

Homemade Carrot Cake Continued

15 minutes and then invert onto tray or cooling rack. Layer and frost.

You can also make these into cupcakes by baking them in cupcake-lined muffin tins. Bake for 15-20 minutes. Check with a knife inserted in center for doneness. Watch closely. Frost with "Dena's Butter Cream Frosting" (page 101) or "Cream Cheese Frosting" (page 109). Yum!

Makes 2 round cakes

Notes

Chocolate Chip Banana Bread

- 1¾ cups flour
- 1 tsp baking soda
- 1 tsp baking powder
- ¼ tsp salt
- ¾ cup semi-sweet chocolate chips
- ¼ cup milk chocolate chips
- 1 cup pecans (finely chopped in food processor)
- 1 stick unsalted butter
- 1¼ cups sugar
- 2 large eggs
- 1 cup mashed bananas
- 1 Tbsp lemon juice
- 1 Tbsp pure vanilla extract

Preheat oven to 350°. Prepare your loaf pans with non stick flour cooking spray. Thoroughly spray your pans (don't be shy with it). Combine all of the dry ingredients in a bowl. In a stand mixer (or hand held mixer) use medium to high speed to beat the softened butter and sugar until fluffy. Add the eggs, bananas, lemon juice, and vanilla extract to the butter mixture. Mix in the combined flour and add the chocolate chips and nuts to the mix. Pour the batter into the prepared loaf pans.

Bake for 45 minutes to 1 hour depending on your oven. Use a knife inserted in the center of the pan to test for doneness. Let cool for 15 minutes and invert the pan onto a cutting board or cooling rack. Slice and enjoy! Great with "Dena's Butter Cream Frosting" (page 101) or some creamy butter!

Makes approximately 12 slices of bread

Notes

Golden Apricot Tea Cookies

- 1 cup of unsalted butter (softened)
- ½ cup sugar
- 1½ tsp pure vanilla extract
- 2½ Tbsp Golden Apricot Tea (place in a food processor and run for 2 minutes)
- 1 Tbsp chopped dried apricots.

Preheat the oven to 350°. Cream the butter and sugar on medium to high speed of a stand mixer. Add vanilla and mix well. Add the flour, tea, and chopped dried apricots and mix until well combined. Scrape the bottom to incorporate all of the ingredients. Mix again on low speed.

Form balls of dough using a small cookie scoop (found at Target®, Walmart®, Kmart®, and kitchen supply stores). You can store the cookie dough balls in freezer safe bags for later use. These are great for surprise guests or last minute get togethers with friends! Pull them from the freezer and let them thaw for 15 minutes. Sprinkle the tops of each cookie with regular sugar and press them lightly with the bottom of a glass. Pop them in the oven for 8-10 minutes. Enjoy! If you want to dress them up you can drizzle white chocolate over them and top with a slice of dried apricot! Yum!

White Chocolate:

Using a microwave safe bowl – pour half of a bag of white chocolate chips into it with 1 tsp vegetable oil or 1 tsp of shortening. Heat in microwave for 30-60 seconds. Keep an

Notes

Golden Apricot Tea Cookies Continued

eye on it as white chocolate burns easily. Stir in-between heating times. Add more oil as needed to make a smooth creamy consistency when you stir it with a spoon. Drizzle over your favorite cookie or cake! Pop in the fridge to firm up the chocolate drizzle on your favorite dessert and then you're ready to serve!

Makes 40 cookies

Notes

Ginger Pumpkin Bread

- 3 cups sugar
- 1 cup vegetable oil
- 4 eggs
- 2 cups pumpkin purée (any brand works but Libby's® is my favorite)
- ½ cup water
- 3½ cups flour
- ½ tsp baking powder
- 2 tsp baking soda
- 1 tsp salt
- 2 tsp cinnamon
- 1 tsp cloves
- 1 tsp nutmeg
- 1 Tbsp powdered ginger
- 1 cup nuts (chopped in food processor)

Optional:
- Add 1 Tbsp chopped candied or crystallized ginger to the mixture for that extra something special.

Preheat oven to 350°.

Combine sugar, oil, eggs, and pumpkin purée in a stand mixer. Add water on low speed. In a separate bowl whisk the dry ingredients together including spices. Turn electric mixer on low speed and slowly add the dry ingredients to the bowl. Add the chopped nuts and candied ginger. Mix on low speed

Notes

Ginger Pumpkin Bread Continued

until everything is well combined. Spray two loaf pans with non stick flour baking spray. Don't be shy with the spray. Coat it very well. Pour the batter into the loaf pans equally. Bake for approximately 1 hour 15 minutes. Keep an eye on the bread as it bakes (ovens vary in temperature and cooking times). When a knife inserted in the center of each loaf comes out clean you are ready to pull it from the oven. Let it rest for 15 minutes and then shake the pan gently to loosen the bread from it. Flip the pan to release the bread to a serving tray. Wonderful with a cup of hot tea on an Autumn day!

Makes 2 large loaves of bread

Notes

Easy Spiced Cupcakes

- 1 spice cake mix (Duncan Hines® is our favorite brand for this recipe)
- 1 pkg vanilla instant pudding
- 1 cup buttermilk
- 4 eggs
- ½ cup vegetable oil
- ½ cup apple juice
- ½ cup currants or raisins (if you don't like raisins – omit them)
- ½ cup chopped pecans or walnuts

Optional:

- ½ cup shredded coconut
- 2 tsp ginger

Preheat oven to 350°. Mix together the cake mix, pudding, buttermilk, eggs, oil, ginger, and apple juice. Beat on medium speed until well combined. Fold in the raisins, nuts, and coconut until well combined. Line muffin tins with some fun cupcake liners. Fill the cupcake liners ½ full. Bake about 10-13 minutes (depending on your oven). Keep a close eye on them. Tap the center of the cupcake lightly with your fingertips. If it springs back lightly it is done. Or use a knife inserted in the center of one to test for doneness. Don't over-bake them as this will cause dry cupcakes. Pull from the oven as soon as they spring back and let rest for 15 minutes. Invert pan onto a cooling rack or cutting board. Let them cool

Notes

Easy Spiced Cupcakes Continued

thoroughly. Using a piping bag frost them with "Dena's Butter Cream Frosting" (page 101) or "Cream Cheese Frosting"
(page 109)! Yum! Garnish with some finely chopped pecans
or walnuts sprinkled on top!

Optionally, garnish the tops with shredded coconut that has
been toasted lightly in the oven for 10-12 minutes at 350°.

Makes approximately 45 cupcakes

Notes

Dena's "Don't Sweat It" Cinnamon Rolls

I love cinnamon rolls but I don't always have the time to make them the old fashioned way with yeast dough. I discovered that substituting cottage cheese for yeast creates a quick dough that tastes very delicious. I hope you enjoy this "Don't Sweat It" version of homemade cinnamon rolls.

- ¾ cup large curd Cottage cheese
- ⅓ cup buttermilk
- ⅓ cup sugar
- 4 Tbsp melted butter (microwave is fine for this)
- 2 cups of flour
- 1 Tbsp. baking powder
- ½ tsp salt
- ¼ tsp baking soda

Filling:
- 1½ Tbsp butter melted
- 1 cup brown sugar
- 2 tsp cinnamon
- 1 tsp nutmeg
- 1 cup chopped walnuts or pecans.

Put all of the above ingredients into a food processor. Pulse it until combined. Don't go crazy with it...just until it holds together. Pull the dough ball from the processor and shape it into a round disk on a lightly floured cutting board. Keep extra flour on hand to sprinkle on the top of the dough

Notes

Dena's "Don't Sweat It" Cinnamon Rolls
Continued

and on your hands. Using a rolling pin start from the middle and gently push the dough out. Try to keep the dough even and in a square shape. You're looking for ¼ inch thickness.

Combine all filling ingredients and sprinkle the over the dough evenly. Roll the dough into a tube starting from one side to the other. Once the dough is in a tube shape slice it in two inch pieces. Spray a baking sheet with non stick flour baking spray (Pam is great). Be generous with the spray to keep it from sticking. Preheat oven to 400°. Lay the slices on their sides so that the filling is visible. Bake for 20-25 minutes (depending on your oven). Watch closely. They will be lightly browned yet soft and delicious. Enjoy with "Dena's Butter Cream Frosting" (page 101) as a topping! Yum!

Makes approximately 1 dozen good size cinnamon rolls

Notes

Dena's "Don't Be Intimidated" Pie Crust

- 3 cups regular flour
- ¼ cup sugar
- 1 stick unsalted butter
- ½ stick of Crisco® Butter Flavored Shortening (use the stick for easy preparation)
- 1 tsp salt
- 1 cup of ice water (not all of the water will be used though)

Tips

- The ice water must be exactly that a cup of water full of ice cubes. This will keep your butter and Crisco very cold in the mixing process and make a flakey crust.
- Don't over handle the dough as it will warm the butter and it will lose its flakey texture.

Place the flour and sugar in the mixing bowl of a stand mixer. Use the paddle attachment. Whisk the dry ingredients together. Add the salt. Cut the butter and Crisco stick into cubes. Add them to the flour mixture and turn the mixer on low speed – then turn it up to medium speed to combine. Wait until the butter and Crisco form small pea size bits. Don't over mix. You still want to see small bits of butter. Slowly stream in the ice water. Add tiny dribbles of the water to the low/medium speed mixer. When the dough begins to form a solid shape stop adding water. You don't want it to be too soft. You want it to barely hold together. Not crumbly though. Turn the dough onto a generously floured cutting board. Separate it into two balls. Press one ball into a

Notes

Dena's "Don't Be Intimidated" Pie Crust Continued

disk shape with your hands. Sprinkle flour over the top of the disk. I like to coat my hands and my rolling pin with flour too. Begin rolling in long strokes. Many people make the mistake of doing lots of little strokes on their pie crust. Long strokes prevent the dough from getting over worked or tear as easily. Once you have rolled the dough out, roll it into a tube and lay on your pie plate. Unroll it to fit perfectly in your pan. You can trim edges with knife or crimp it to the proper size you want. If you want a double crust follow the same procedure with the second ball of dough and lay over your favorite pie filling. Crimp edges together and poke vent holes for proper cooking. Cover the edge of your pie crust with foil or the new crust covers (found at most kitchen supply stores). We love ours for baking "Roasted Red Pepper and Artichoke Quiche" (page 25)! Enjoy!

Makes enough for a double crust

Notes

Chris' Classic Chocolate Peanut Butter Spread

Chris Jennings roots are from the Midwest. She grew up enjoying wonderful family favorites such as this spread recipe. Her mom would toast bread and spread chocolate peanut butter and a fresh leaf of lettuce to make these tasty sandwiches.

This spread would also be a great condiment for simple butter scones.

- 4 Tbsp cocoa powder
- 8 Tbsp sugar
- 8 Tbsp unsalted butter (lightly melted in microwave)
- 2 tsp pure vanilla extract
- 8 oz. peanut butter

Melt the butter slightly (35-40 seconds in microwave), add cocoa powder, sugar, peanut butter, and vanilla extract and mix until creamy and smooth. Use a stand or hand mixer to make it smooth and creamy.

Notes

Dena's Butter Cream Frosting

- 2 cups of unsalted butter (thoroughly softened the old fashioned way...set out on counter for 2 hours)
- 3 cups of powdered sugar
- 1 Tbsp pure vanilla extract
- 3 Tbsp of whole milk

The secret to making great butter cream frosting is the butter itself. Please use good quality unsalted butter and let it soften completely outside of the refrigerator.

If you like a "sweet and salty" frosting, you can substitute salted butter for the unsalted. I actually love this contrasting flavor.

If you plan to make your frosting in the afternoon put it out on your counter first thing in the morning. You can even let it sit out overnight without fear of it spoiling for preparing it first thing in the morning. The golden rule: it needs to be thoroughly softened. Microwaving is not a good method as it softens portions of the butter too much while others are still too firm and chunky. Do it the old fashioned way and you will be pleased with the results.

You need a stand mixer or hand mixer to get the best consistency.

Add the softened butter to your mixing bowl. Use the beater bar to cream the butter first. Change to the whisk paddle and add the powdered sugar. Whisk on low speed first to combine with the butter. Then add your vanilla extract and

Notes

Dena's Butter Cream Frosting Continued

your whole milk. Mix until its smooth and creamy. Flip the switch to high power! Let it run for 3-5 minutes. It will be nice and fluffy! You are now ready to scoop it into a piping bag fitted with a medium tip. Pipe this butter cream frosting onto your favorite cupcake and enjoy!

Makes 4 cups of homemade butter cream frosting!

Easily frosts 30 cupcakes!

Notes

Dena's Créme Brule Custard

- 9 egg yolks
- 1 cup sugar
- 1 quart heavy whipping cream
- 2 tsp pure vanilla extract

Preheat oven to 325°. In a bowl whisk together the sugar with egg yolks until thick and smooth. Pour heavy whipping cream into a microwave safe bowl and heat in the microwave for 1 minute. Whisk and heat an additional 30 - 50 seconds (until the cream feels warm but not overly hot – watch closely). Temper the yolks by adding the warm cream slowly – whisking as you combine. Add the 2 tsp of pure vanilla extract to the mixture. Whisk thoroughly.

It's helpful to put the mixture into a pitcher at this point. Place as many custard cups as you can into a 13 x 9 inch deep baking dish (you may need two pans). Leave ½ inch space between the custard cups. Pour the custard batter into the cups at least ¾ full. Pour cold water into the 13 x 9 pan to cover approximately half way up the custard cups. Bake until set. Approximately 40 minutes. Check after 30 minutes. You may want to rotate your pan to make for even cooking. If the custard is still soft to the touch yet is browning too quickly cover it with some foil toward the end of baking time.

Remove from oven and let stand until room temperature. Remove from water bath and place in the fridge to chill for 2 hours. You can sprinkle with brown sugar and torch (with a special Créme Brule lighter) or broil for a brief time in your oven. I like to top mine with a fresh raspberry! Serve and enjoy!

Makes approximately 2 dozen small custard cups

Notes

"Everything but the Kitchen Sink" Shortbread Tea Cookies

- 2 cups unsalted butter
- 1 cup sugar
- 3¾ cups flour
- 2 tsp vanilla
- ¼ cup mini semi-sweet chocolate chips
- ¼ cup white chips
- ¼ cup raisins or currants
- ¼ cup slivered raw almonds
- ¼ cup honey grahams (pulsed up in a food processor)

Soften the butter on the counter for 20 minutes. Place softened butter into a stand mixer bowl. Add the 1 cup sugar and whip until fluffy in texture on medium–high speed for 2 minutes. Add the vanilla. Mix well. Add the flour 1 cup at a time on low speed until fully combined. Add in the remaining ingredients (semi-sweet chips, white chips, raisins, raw almonds, and crushed honey grahams). Run on low-medium speed until well combined.

Line cookie sheets with parchment paper. Place scooped cookie dough on baking sheet and sprinkle lightly with regular sugar. Press lightly with a glass to lightly flatten. Bake for 8-9 minutes at 350°. Cookies should be lightly browned.

Garnish with melted chocolate chips mixed with a small amount of vegetable oil. Heat about ¼ cup chocolate chips in microwave for 30-60 seconds with ½ tsp oil. Whisk with fork and drizzle on cookies.

Makes approximately 70 cookies

Notes

Cream Cheese Frosting

If there are comments, they go here

- 2 (8 ounce) packages cream cheese (softened on counter for 2 hours)
- 2 sticks of butter (softened on counter for 2 hours)
- 2½ cups powdered sugar
- 1 Tbsp. orange zest

Place the cream cheese and softened butter into a mixing bowl with a paddle attachment. Beat on high speed for 2 minutes. Add the powdered sugar and orange zest to the mixture and run on low speed until combined.

Switch attachments to the whisk beater. Whisk on high and run for 3 minutes until light and fluffy.

Use on your favorite cake, bread, cinnamon rolls, cupcakes, etc!

Notes

Scones

Peanut Butter Chocolate Chip Scones

- 3 cups self rising flour
- 10 Tbsp cold unsalted butter (cubed)
- ½ cup sugar
- 4 Tbsp peanut butter (creamy or chunky – your preference)
- 1 cup plus 2 Tbsp buttermilk
- ½ cup semi-sweet chocolate chips

Mix together flour and sugar. Add to the food processor. Cut in 10 Tbsp cold unsalted butter (pre cubed). Pulse until it resembles coarse cornmeal. Pour into a large mixing bowl. Add the 4 Tbsp of peanut butter and chocolate chips. Fold into flour mixture with a large rubber spatula until the dough just barely holds together. Turn dough onto a floured cutting board (we like using a large wooden board). Pat into a large circle that is one inch thick. Cut into triangles and place on a parchment lined baking sheet. Bake at 350° for 14-20 minutes (depending on your oven). Watch closely as they bake. Check for a light brown on the bottom of the scones. Pull and let rest. Prepare your glaze now.

Glaze:

Mix 1 cup powdered sugar with 3 Tbsp Peanut Butter and just enough milk (2-3 Tbsp milk approximately). This will make a creamy smooth glaze topping. Drizzle on top of the scones for a rich scone or leave them plain. Delicious as a dessert scone.

Makes 7 scones

Notes

Honey Spiced Scones

- 3 cups self rising flour
- ¾ cups sugar
- ½ cup butter
- 1 teabag opened of Good Earth® "Sweet and Spicy Tea"
- 1 cup buttermilk
- 3 Tbsp honey

Mix together flour and sugar. Use a food processor for easy preparation. Add the flour mixture and the 1 teabag of "Sweet and Spicy tea" to the food processor and add the cubed cold butter to the mixture. Pulse the flour mixture in the processor until crumbly like course cornmeal. Place the mixture in a large mixing bowl. Add half of the buttermilk to the flour/butter/tea mixture. Fold the mixture with a large rubber spatula to combine. Be very careful not to over mix the dough as this will make it tough. Add the 3-4 Tbsp of honey at this point. Fold the honey in to combine it. Keep adding the buttermilk in small amounts until all the flour is combined and not too dry, but barely holds together. You don't want it too moist as it will make hard scones. Turn dough out onto a floured cutting board and pat gently into a circle (about 1 inch thick) and cut into triangles and place on a parchment lined baking sheet. Bake at 350° for 14 – 20 minutes. Every oven varies in baking time and temperature. Watch them closely for light browning on the bottom of the scones. Pull from oven and let them rest.

Glaze:

Mix together 1 cup of powdered sugar, 2 Tbsp water, 1-2 tsp of honey. Dip or drizzle the glaze onto the top of slightly cooled scones. Let set and serve. Makes 8 scones

Notes

Chris' Pumpkin Cream Cheese Scones

- 9 cups self-rising flour
- 3 Sticks of unsalted COLD butter
- 1½ cups sugar
- 3 cups buttermilk
- 1 15 ounce can solid pack pumpkin purée (no spices)
- 1 8 ounce container whipped cream cheese
- 1 tsp pumpkin pie (or apple pie) spice
- 1 tsp cinnamon

Place 1 cup of self rising flour into a food processor with the cubed 3 sticks of very cold butter. Pulse to create a corn meal consistency. Move the pulsed flour/butter mixture in to a large mixing bowl and add the remaining 8 cups of self rising flour plus the 1 ½ cups of sugar. Mix well with a large, rubber spatula. Add the pie spice and cinnamon to the mixture. Fully combine. Fold in the pumpkin purée until well combined. Begin pouring in the buttermilk one cup at a time. Using a folding technique combine the buttermilk with the flour mixture. Be careful not to overwork the dough or get it too moist. The last step is to fold in the 8 ounce container of whipped cream cheese. This will create a marbleized texture in the scone dough.

Turn dough out onto a lightly floured cutting board and pat gently into a circle (about 1 inch thick) and cut into triangles. Place on a parchment lined baking sheet. Bake at 350° for 14-20 minutes depending upon your oven temperature

Notes

Chris' Pumpkin Cream Cheese Scones
Continued

variation. Watch them closely for light browning on the bottoms. Pull from the oven and let them rest to cool. Dip or drizzle them with the following glaze.

Glaze:

3 cups powdered sugar, 1 tsp cinnamon, add enough water to whisk into a drizzling consistency over the tops of the scones.

Makes 27–30 scones

Notes

Index

Index Continued

Also from ATR Publishing

Creating an Afternoon to Remember

A Little of This and a Little of That

Making It Your Own Afternoon to Remember

Tea Time Tidbits and Treats

Drop by for Tea

Master Tea Room Recipes

Order them online at
http://www.afternoontoremember.com/